T0010570

The Legend of the Torch Festival

By Sunshine Orange Studio
Translated by Dai Rongheng
Adapted by Joe Gregory

Books Beyond Boundaries

ROYAL COLLINS

The Legend of the Torch Festival

By Sunshine Orange Studio
Translated by Dai Rongheng
Adapted by Joe Gregory

First published in 2022 by Royal Collins Publishing Group Inc.
Groupe Publication Royal Collins Inc.
BKM Royalcollins Publishers Private Limited

Headquarters: 550-555 boul. René-Lévesque O Montréal (Québec) H2Z1B1 Canada
India office: 805 Hemkunt House, 8th Floor, Rajendra Place, New Delhi 110 008

Original Edition © Yunnan Education Publishing House Co., Ltd.

All rights reserved. Without limiting the rights under copyright reserved above, no part of this publication may be reproduced, stored in or introduced into a retrieval system, or transmitted in any form or by any means (electronic, mechanical, photocopying, recording or otherwise), without the prior written permission of both the copyright owner and the above publisher of this book.

ISBN: 978-1-4878-1017-7

To find out more about our publications, please visit www.royalcollins.com.

A long, long time ago, there was a god named Sire Abi. He had the strength to move mountains and he was stronger than all the other gods, something he was very proud of.

In the human world, there was also a man born with the great strength. His name was Atilaba, and he often used his strength to help other people, earning the love and praise of those around him.

Sire Abi heard of Atilaba's unusual strength and great capabilities. So he decided to come down to earth from Heaven. He wanted to compare himself with Atilaba and he wanted to do so by wrestling him.

After hearing of the god's challenge, Atilaba made a plan for how to beat Sire Abi. As Atilaba was in a hurry to leave, he said to his mother, "Mother, a man from Heaven with great strength will come to compete with me. Please prepare him a meal made with hot pieces of iron. Tell him that it is my favorite food and let him try them." With these words, Atilaba left home.

Soon, Sire Abi arrived at Atilaba's home. Just as her son had asked her, Atilaba's mother treated Sire Abi to a bowl of hot iron pieces.

Sire Abi put a piece of iron in his mouth, but he could not chew it. He thought to himself, "If Atilaba eats iron, he must be stronger than me!" With this thought, Sire Abi made an excuse to leave and hurried back to Heaven.

Soon, Atilaba came back and his mother told him what had happened. When Atilaba heard that Sire Abi could not chew the iron, he was convinced that Sire Abi was not stronger than him. So he went to look for Sire Abi.

Just as Sire Abi was returning to Heaven, Atilaba
caught up with him. Atilaba yelled, "Don't go!
You want to fight me, so let's go!"

Atilaba's words angered the arrogant Sire Abi. He flung his arms around Atilaba's waist, attempting to throw Atilaba to the ground. But Atilaba would not let Sire Abi succeed. So, he squatted down, steadied his feet, grabbed Sire Abi's shoulders, and pushed him down.

They both had great strength and roared loudly as they stomped the ground, making the trees shake and the mountains tremble.

Trying to catch Atilaba off guard, Sire Abi suddenly grabbed Atilaba, attempting to slam him into the ground. Atilaba stumbled and was almost pinned to the ground by Sire Abi.

But to Sire Abi's surprise, Atilaba jumped up into the air, made a smooth somersault, and finally landed on Sire Abi's back. Sire Abi was defeated! But he refused to accept defeat, and asked for a rematch.

This time, Atilaba planted his feet down on the ground and bent his legs slightly. Sire Abi used all his strength to put Atilbala off balance. Still, Atilaba's feet stayed rooted to the ground and his body did not move the slightest bit.

Suddenly, Atilaba took advantage of Sire Abi's carelessness, grabbed his arm and threw him in the air. Sire Abi landed a short distance away, with his face down on the ground. Sire Abi did not move, so Atilaba carefully went over to take a look. As he got closer, he saw that Sire Abi was dead.

The gods were in a great rage when they saw Sire Abi being slammed to his death. But as they could not find a way to punish Atilaba directly, they sent a swarm of locusts to eat all the people's crops.

All this happened on the 24th day of the sixth month of the lunar calendar and on that evening, Atilaba cut a branch from a pine tree to make a torch and led the villagers to drive away the locusts.

The torches burned for three days and three nights. Finally the people drove away all the locusts and saved the crops.

The Yi people gathered together and rejoiced,
singing and dancing and celebrating their victory.

Since then, the Yi people have celebrated the Torch Festival on the 24th of the sixth month of the lunar calendar. During the festival, they use flint stones to light their torches in the traditional way and walk to the fields to pray for a good harvest in the coming year.